Buddhism
for Bears

D1395435

Buddhism for Bears

Illustrated by Chris Riddell

Text by Claire Nielson

EBURY PRESS
LONDON

First published in 1998

5 7 9 10 8 6 4

Text copyright © Claire Nielson 1998
Illustrations copyright © Chris Riddell 1998

Chris Riddell has asserted his right to be identified as illustrator of this work.

First published in the United Kingdom in 1998 by Ebury Press
Random House · 20 Vauxhall Bridge Road · London SW1V 2SA

Random House Australia (Pty) Limited
20 Alfred Street · Milsons Point · Sydney · New South Wales 2061 · Australia

Random House New Zealand Limited
18 Poland Road · Glenfield · Auckland 10 · New Zealand

Random House South Africa (Pty) Limited
Endulini · 5a Jubilee Road · Parktown 2193 · South Africa

The Random House Group Limited Reg. No. 954009

www.randomhouse.co.uk

A CIP catalogue record for this book is available from the British Library

ISBN 0 09 186504 2

Designed by Lovelock & Co

Printed and bound in Great Britain by Mackays of Chatham plc, Kent

Contents

Wisdom

Ask yourself, what is power?

Experience life as a flowing movement

Keep in touch with the here and now

It is unwise to eat to
one's utmost capacity

Endeavour to find the one behind the many

Let go of the craving and greed ...

... that bind you to the world

There are skilled and unskilled states of mind

Love other living beings as members of the universe

Banish interests and activities opposed
to the ideal of enlightenment

Self-Control

Refrain from taking
what has not been given

Avoid the distinctive …

... and the superficial

Abstain from drinking intoxicating liquors and spirits

Abstain from non-celibacy

Even in dreams do not
commit unwholesome
offences

Have no use for luxurious beds and seats

Practice self-restraint with regard to your fellow beings

Do not squander energy in the
foolish pursuit of the inconsequential

Techniques

For meditation select a room
that is quiet, clean and tidy

Sitting is the foundation of meditation

Sit with a sense of gratitude and dignity

You may experience the dropping-off of body and mind

Beginners in meditation should not sit for too long a time

The lotus position may hurt the beginner's legs

Always adopt an erect sitting position when meditating

Endeavour to experience each breath you take in and out

Liberate the spirit

Endeavour to make the mind void

Do not allow your mind to become dull or lax

Choose nourishing vegetables …

... rather than meat

Vigorous body movements may
evoke a feeling of wellbeing

Seek to govern your behaviour by the
principle of non-violence

Principles of behaviour may be transmitted
from teachers to disciple

Demonstrate a spirit of tenderness towards others

Practice complete awareness of body,
thoughts and feelings

Cultivate a profound silence
in the deepest recesses of the mind

Constantly question how to live in the
world and yet find liberation

Truth

At certain points during meditation you will
suddenly have insights about yourself

All is equally holy, be it diamonds or dung

The perfect way knows no difficulties

Demonstrate reality rather than discuss it

The true nature of the void remains unknown

Existence is a never-ending flow of change

The inner being should not
be shackled to the body

Renounce all worldly things

Self-mortification does not lead to inner truth

Be ready for the
great awakening

Remember to allow the law
of karma to regulate all activities